CITIZENS UNITED[1]

Since the landmark 2010 *Citizens United v Federal Election Commission* case[2], which ruled that campaign expenditure limits and restrictions on the broadcast of electioneering communications are unconstitutional violations of the First Amendment protection of political speech, the floodgates to have opened to corporations to donate to Super PACs and fund multi-billion dollar federal elections to Congress and the Presidency of the United States. There has been a massive public backlash against this ruling by American citizens of all political persuasions, working through grassroots organizations, petitions to Congress, town hall meetings, and public demonstrations and protests. The State legislatures of California, Colorado, Connecticut, Delaware, Hawaii, Illinois, Maine, Maryland, Massachusetts, Montana, New Jersey, New Mexico, Oregon, Rhode Island, Vermont, and West Virginia have passed state constitutional amendments or resolutions to Congress to call a National Convention under Article V of the Constitution to amend it. These States have called on Congress to amend the Constitution to establish unequivocally that the enumerated rights belong to natural persons and not corporations, which are artificial creatures defined by law to conduct commerce or public works as a single commercial entity acting on behalf of a group of persons. Many other states are writing their own amendments and resolutions. Since 2010, over a dozen resolutions, bills, and constitutional amendments have been proposed by members of the House and Senate. After several attempts to get a bill or resolution out of committee, Tom Udall (D-NM) along with 48 co-sponsors, finally introduced S.J. Res 19 to the Senate, where on the 11th September, 2014, after receiving 54-42 vote on the floor, a Republican filibuster blocked it. The text of this resolution read,

That the following article is proposed as an amendment to the Constitution of the United States, which shall be valid to all intents and purposes as part of the Constitution when ratified by the legislatures of three-fourths of the several States:

1. To advance democratic self-government and political equality, and to protect the integrity of government and the electoral process, Congress and the States may regulate and set reasonable limits on the raising and spending of money by candidates and others to influence elections.
2. Congress and the States shall have power to implement and enforce this article by appropriate legislation, and may distinguish between natural persons and corporations or other artificial entities created by law, including by prohibiting such entities from spending money to influence elections.
3. Nothing in this article shall be construed to grant Congress or the States the power to abridge the freedom of the press.

Udall's latest attempt to pass this amendment is S.J. Res 5, which (since January 21, 2015) has been under consideration by the Senate Judiciary Committee. There are currently eight proposed House joint resolutions and three Senate joint resolutions in committees, all seeking to amend the Constitution to define persons as natural persons or clarify Congress's authority to legislate elections, and limit campaign contributions and expenditures. Meanwhile, after the record breaking $2 billion presidential campaign of 2014, with the prospects of even greater expenditure for the 2016 presidential election, big money continues to flow into American politics, and there seems little movement towards overturning the Supreme Court. Why did this landmark ruling occur and what are its implications for the electoral process?

Historical background:

In the run up to the 2004 George W. Bush v John Kerry presidential election, a complaint was made to the Federal Election Commission (FEC) on behalf of a non-profit corporation named Citizens United about the airing of advertisements for Michael Moore's *Fahrenheit 9/11*. The complaint was that because of Moore's portrayal of Bush and Cheney as war criminals, who should be impeached and jailed rather than re-elected (if they really had been elected in the first place), such ads constituted "electioneering communications" against Bush, and that they should not be aired during the 60 days prior to the election, in accordance with 2002 Bipartisan Campaign Reform Act. The FEC ruled against Citizens United on the grounds that Moore's movie was a commercial product for sale, either by paying to see it in a movie theater or buying a DVD, and ads for the movie were legitimate commercials selling a product and not "electioneering communications." In response to this ruling, Citizens United put together *Hillary: The Movie*[3] to be aired on pay-for-view DirecTV the night before the 2008 Democratic Party primaries. This was blocked by the FEC who, along with the United States Court for the District of Columbia, ruled that the movie was a partisan attack ad and an "electioneering communication." *Hillary: The Movie* could not be aired the night before the primaries began.

Citizens United did not let the matter rest. With the support of the U.S. Chamber of Commerce and the National Rifle Association, Citizens United took the matter before the courts. It came before SCOTUS on March, 24th, 2009. Rather than simply deliberate on whether the FEC had acted inconsistently, arbitrarily, or had overstepped its authority in this particular instance, as the petitioner had complained, SCOTUS took the initiative and decide to deliberate on the much wider question of the constitutionally of provisions of BCRA limiting expenditures, as well as restrictions on showing electioneering communications in the run up to primaries and elections, as possible violations of the First Amendment right to freedom of speech, especially political speech. On June 29, 2009, SCOTUS directed the parties to prepare to reargue their case on September 9, with this wider question in mind, and on January 21, 2010, SCOTUS decided in favor of Citizens United and ruled BCRA unconstitutional.

This case should not be viewed in isolation. To understand why *Citizens United v FEC* was a landmark ruling it needs to be viewed in historical context. BCRA was not the first campaign reform legislation to come out of Congress, and it was not the first to be brought before SCOTUS. For the last 150 years, Congress has attempted to legislate limits to campaign financing and maintain at least the appearance of electoral integrity and legitimacy. It started in 1867 when an amendment to the Naval Appropriations Bill prohibited federal officers and employees from soliciting donations from Navy Yard workers. This was done to prevent workers from being shaken down with the threat of losing their jobs if they did not "donate" part of their wages. In 1883, this was expanded by the Civil Service Reform Act to prohibit any government official or employee from soliciting donations from any federal civil workers and governmental employees. After the scandal and controversy about political patronage and corruption during the 1896 presidential campaign between William McKinley and William Jennings Bryan, in which McKinley alone reported to have raised and spent an unprecedented $16 million, with at least half coming directly from corporations with an interest in McKinley's call for protective trade tariffs and his opposition to the issuance of silver coin to secure the value of bank notes (which would prevent banks from lending more than their reserves), there was widespread public demand for Congress to reform campaign financing and put an end to blatant cronyism, patronage, and corruption. In response to this public demand, during the 1904 presidential campaign Theodore Roosevelt called for campaign funding reform and for the prohibition of donations from corporations, which he reiterated in his first State of the Union address to Congress in 1905. Not only did Roosevelt call on Congress to prohibit corporations from contributing money to any political committee or for any political purpose, but he also called for a law preventing corporate directors from using stockholders' money for political purposes. While the stockholders would remain at liberty to donate their own money as they wished, corporate directors should not be able to use that money for them *without shareholders consent* for the purposes of "donations" (i.e. bribes) to corrupt public officials and politicians. In 1907, Congress passed and Roosevelt signed the Tillman Act, which explicitly prohibited donations from corporations and banks to any political party or candidate for any federal office, including Congress and the Presidency.

Over the next century, Congress wrote and passed a series of laws, amendments, repeals, and reforms, largely to close loopholes and fix flaws in the previous efforts, all with the explicit aims of establishing comprehensive regulation of campaign financing, deterring corruption and the appearance of corruption; providing public funds for general elections; educating the electorate; increasing voter suffrage and registration; and preserving the appearance of the integrity of the electoral process and the legitimacy of representative government. Since the Tillman Act, these laws have set limits on contributions from wealthy individuals and special interest groups, and prohibited corporations and banks from donating at all. This was done with the explicit aim of preventing moneyed interests from having a disproportionate influence on national elections and undermining the democratic process. In 1910 Congress passed the Federal Corrupt Practices Act (FCPA), which enacted spending limits on campaigns for election to the House of Representatives. In 1911 it was amended to include the Senate as well (the next national election and first direct popular election of senators occurred in 1914) and placed disclosure requirements on the sources of donations to both parties and candidates for election to Congress. These restrictions on contributions and expenditures, and donation disclosure requirements, were strengthened in 1925 by the further amendments of the FCPA, and in 1939 (and again in 1940) by the Hatch Act, which set individual contribution limits to $5,000 per year to a political party or candidate, and also asserted the right of Congress to regulate primary elections. All contributions of $50 and over during a calendar year had to be reported, and senatorial candidates could spend no more than three cents for each voter in the last election, to a maximum of $25,000. House candidates could also spend up to three cents per voter in the last election, up to a $5,000 maximum. Offers of patronage and contracts were banned, as were any form of bribery. Corporate contributions of all kinds were banned. The 1935 Public Utilities Holdings Act prohibited public utilities from donating to political campaigns. The 1947 Taft-Hartley Act extended to prohibition on candidates and parties from accepting donations for federal elections from labor unions as well as corporations and banks.

Unfortunately, however, these laws were poorly enforced because Congress had failed to provide any institutional framework to oversee their enforcement, and congressmen, parties, and candidates were left to police themselves. As a result, the restrictions on campaign financing were largely ignored. Amendments to these laws had already lifted spending limits, except when campaign committees were active in two or more States, and candidates could avoid the spending limit and disclosure requirements altogether if they claimed to have no knowledge of how campaign donations were being spent. Arguably, these laws were cosmetic and little more than populist and opportunistic efforts to gain votes on the back of public sentiment and outrage rather than genuine attempts at campaign reform, but they maintained the appearance of political transparency and integrity, all the while politicians and party apparatchiks failed to report donations and accepted bribes in exchange for promises of favor and contracts. In 1966, President Lyndon B. Johnson referred to the FCPA as "more loophole than law."

In response to criticisms and failures of the FCPA, Congress passed and President Richard Nixon signed into law the 1971 Federal Elections Campaign Act (FECA), alongside the 1971 Revenue Act, which required full reporting of campaign contributions and expenditures, as well as giving broad definitions of both, with the aim of strictly prohibiting patronage and the promise of patronage. It prohibited contracts between any candidate for federal office and any federal department or agency. It set strict caps on the amounts individuals (and their family members) could contribute to their own campaigns—$50 thousand for presidential and vice-presidential candidates, $35 thousand for Senate candidates, and $25 thousand for House candidates. Congressional candidates had reported raising and spending $9 million during the 1968 election, but, after the enactment of FECA, candidates reported that they raised and spent almost $90 million in the run up to the 1972 election.[4] FECA had laid out a framework for enforcement, and the result was the congressmen and parties were much more careful about disclosing sources and amounts. Initially, it did not provide for a single, independent agency or committee to monitor and enforce the law, instead giving authority to three offices, the Clerk of the House, the Secretary of the Senate, and the Comptroller General of the United States General Accounting Office (GAO), each independently monitoring compliance with FECA and referring violations of the law to the Department of Justice. In 1974, FECA was amended to create the FEC as a single government agency responsible for overseeing FECA and reporting violations to the DOJ. As well as responsibility for monitoring compliance with FECA, the FEC was given jurisdiction in civil enforcement matters, authority to write regulations, and serve as a national clearinghouse for information on the administration of elections.

FECA set a cap on television advertising expenditure at 10 cents per voter in the last election, or $50 thousand, whichever is higher. In 1973, Congress enacted a provision of the Revenue Act that allowed citizens to check a box on their tax forms authorizing the Treasury to use $1 to finance public funding of presidential campaigns. The 1974 amendments provided for partial public funding, in the form of matching funds, for presidential primary candidates, and also extended public funding to political parties to finance their presidential nominating conventions. By 1976 the fund was large enough for the 1976 election to be the first publicly-funded federal election in U.S. history.

However, FECA also opened the door to donations from corporations and unions by allowing the formation of segregated funds, or political action committees (PACs), to collect voluntary donations from employees and union members to donate to federal elections. Individual contributions to national political parties were limited to $20 thousand per year, and individual contributions to a PAC to $5 thousand per year. The 1939 prohibition on accepting donations from federal contractors was also relaxed. Both corporations and unions with federal contracts could also set up and run PACs. This law permitted corporate PACs to solicit employees as well as its stockholders. The 1976 amendments imposed significant restrictions on PAC solicitations by specifying who could be solicited and how solicitations should be conducted. In addition, a single contribution limit was adopted for all PACs established by the same union or corporation.

FECA was immediately challenged as unconstitutional in the Supreme Court by Senator James L. Buckley (R-NY) and Eugene McCarthy (D-MN) against Francis R. Valeo, the Secretary of the Senate. This resulted in the 1976 *Buckley v. Valeo* (424 U.S. 1, 1976) ruling that expenditure limits were an unconstitutional violation of the First Amendment protection of free speech, except when presidential candidates accepted public funding. SCOTUS also ruled that limits on candidates spending their own money was unconstitutional. In short, SCOTUS assumed that money is speech. However, the SCOTUS majority ruling upheld the limits on contributions, public funding provisions, and the disclosure requirements. SCOTUS also ruled that the method of appointing FEC commissioners violated the constitutional principle of separation of powers, since commissioners had executive powers, but Congress, not the President, appointed four of the commissioners. After this ruling, FECA was amended such that expenditure limits were repealed (except for candidates receiving public funds) and henceforth the President appointed the commission members and the Senate confirmed them. SCOTUS later formally restated that expenditure limits were constitutional for presidential candidates receiving public funds in *RNC v. FEC* (445 U.S. 955, 1980). FECA was further amended in 1979, 1982, 1983, and 1984 to simplify reporting requirements, extend public funding to state and local levels, and increase public funding for presidential nominating committees. The new amendments also prohibited the FEC from conducting random campaign audits, allowed state and local parties to spend unlimited amounts on federal campaign efforts (including the production and distribution of campaign materials such as signs and bumper stickers used in "get out and vote" drives), and allowed "soft money" donations and contributions that are essentially unregulated providing they are only used "party building" expenses. This amendment allowed corporations, labor unions, and wealthy individuals to contribute as much as they wanted to political parties.

In 1990, in *Austin v. Michigan Chamber of Commerce* (494 U.S. 652) SCOTUS upheld the Michigan Campaign Finance Act's prohibition on corporate donations in support of or opposition to candidates running for the state legislature if that money was not in a segregated fund (PAC). SCOTUS ruled in favor of the State's law prohibition on the Michigan Chamber of Commerce paying for newspaper advertisements from its general fund, rather than only from its segregated fund. The Court agreed 7-2 that MCFA was constitutional. The two dissenting justices were Antonin Scalia (appointed by Ronald Reagan in 1886) and Anthony Kennedy (appointed by Ronald Reagan in 1988). They argued that segregated funds were unconstitutional, and corporations and other such entities should be able to spend their money on political activities without any limits or restraints. They had to wait twenty years before they could overturn these limits and restraints.

Unsurprisingly, after the formation of PACs, the cost of campaigning for federal election increased dramatically. According to the Campaign Finance Institute analysis of FEC data, in 1980 Jimmy Carter and Ronald Reagan each received $29 million dollars in public funds, spending in total $92 million, whereas total campaign spending on the 1988 election between George H. Bush and Michael Dukakis more than doubled to $210 million.[5] In 1980, the total reported expenditure for election to the House was $115 million and by 1988 it had almost doubled to $225 million.[6] The total reported expenditure for election to the Senate was $74 million in 1980 and more than doubled to $185 million by 1988.[7] In 1980 just over 2 thousand PACs were created (1,317 by corporations and 225 by unions, the rest by trade associations or unconnected groups) and by 1988 this number had risen to 3300 PACs (1,600 by corporations and 256 by unions).[8] By the year 2000, for the presidential election campaign between George W. Bush and Al Gore, the total expenditure for the presidential election was $343 million; the total reported expenditure for election to the House had risen to almost $400 million; the total reported expenditure for election to the Senate had risen to $385 million.

In 2002, the Bipartisan Campaign Reform Act (BCRA) was passed by Congress and signed into law by George W. Bush. It was dubbed the "McCain-Feingold Act" after its two Senate sponsors, John McCain (R-AZ) and Russ Feingold (D-WI). Largely supplanting FECA, BCRA prohibited political parties from raising "soft money" (unregulated contributions for party building, voter outreach, etc.) from wealthy donors. Corporations and unions had to form a PAC and allocate segregated funds to political campaigns. PAC expenditures were not limited. The legislation also raised the limits on "hard money" (direct donations to candidates), banned donations from minors, and defined and placed restrictions on "issue advertising," where organizations not directly affiliated with a candidate run "issues ads" that promote or attack specific candidates. BCRA defined political advertising and issue advocacy ads as "electioneering communication" and placed restrictions on how they could be funded and when they could be shown. Henceforth all electioneering communications must identify their sponsor. All broadcast stations were required to sell airtime at its lowest price, and collect and disclose records of purchases made for the purpose of electioneering communication. The BCRA provided an exception to the above for "nonprofit corporations," allowing them to fund electioneering activities and communications, providing that they remained subject to disclosure requirements and did not receive donations from corporations or labor unions.

It is against this historical background that we can see why *Citizens United v. FEC* was a landmark ruling. The 5-4 SCOTUS majority ruled that the First Amendment allows both corporations and unions unlimited expenditure through non-profit organizations as well as funds collected through PACs to pay for the broadcast of issue advocacy ads and electioneering communications, and that there should not be restrictions on when they can be shown.[9] Justice Anthony Kennedy, joined by Chief Justice John Roberts and Justices Samuel Alito, Antonin Scalia, and Clarence Thomas, authored the majority opinion. The majority ruled that the BCRA prohibition of campaign expenditure by corporations and unions on issue advocacy ads and electioneering communications that mention candidates by name during the run up to primaries and elections was in violation of the First Amendment. They claimed that, supposedly since there was no way of distinguishing between media corporations and other kinds of corporation, any such restriction would allow the government to censor the free press and political speech, as media corporations would be prohibited from critically reporting on candidates in the run up to primaries and elections. More specifically, this ruling struck down the BCRA prohibition on any broadcast satellite or cable communication of an issue advocacy ad or "electioneering communication" mentioning a candidate by name from being aired within 60 days before a general election or 30 days before a primary. After this ruling, anyone, any corporation or union, or any organization, as well as collecting donations through a PAC, could also form a non-profit corporation and spend any amount of money on airing political criticism of candidates—even blatant attack ads, slander, and propaganda—during political primaries and campaigns for election to federal office. The majority held that non-profit corporations like Citizens United should continue to disclose their donors, and the federal ban on hard money contributions from corporations or unions to candidates and political parties should remain in effect. Justice Thomas added that he would have also struck down the disclosure and reporting requirements of BCRA in order to protect the anonymity of contributors to protect them from possible retaliation from elected officials.

This case overturned over a century of campaign finance law. It also overturned court precedents such as 1990 *Austin v Michigan Chamber of Commerce*, 1990, when SCOTUS upheld the Michigan Campaign Finance Act that prohibited corporations from using corporate funds to support or oppose a candidate, and *McConnell v FEC*, 2003, when SCOTUS upheld BCRA's extension of FECA to include the categories of issue advocacy ad and electioneering communication as restricted forms of communication during election campaigns and primaries. Roberts recognized that this ruling flew in the face of the legal principle of *stare decisis*[10] and listed the past cases in which SCOTUS had ruled against precedent in his justificatory remarks. The Roberts majority knew what they were doing.

Justice John Paul Stevens wrote the dissent. He was joined by Justices Ruth Bader Ginsburg, Stephen Breyer, and Sonia Sotomayor. Stevens dissented on the grounds that the SCOTUS majority had chosen to hear argument on issues that the litigants had not themselves brought before the court. He claimed that the majority had seized upon the opportunity to make a decision on constitutional grounds when it should have been made on narrower grounds, and stated that the majority "changed the case to give themselves an opportunity to change the law." In other words, he accused the majority of judicial activism. He went further to state that the majority's decision "threatens to undermine the integrity of elected institutions across the nation" and concluded that the majority opinion rejected "the common sense of the American people" who have recognized "a need to prevent corporations from undermining self-government since the founding, and who have fought against the distinctive corrupting potential of corporate electioneering since the days of Theodore Roosevelt." The judicial activism of the SCOTUS majority had thrown out over a century of congressional efforts at campaign reform and court precedent. While Stevens acknowledged that "American democracy is imperfect," he pointed out that few people apart from the majority would have thought that "a dearth of corporate money in politics" was among its flaws.

Justices Scalia, Alito, and Thomas wrote a concurring opinion to address Stevens's dissent. They claimed that the dissenting opinion was "in splendid isolation from the text of the First Amendment" and did not explain why freedom of speech "did not include the freedom to speak in association with other individuals, including association in the corporate form." Scalia, Alito, and Thomas observed that the First Amendment is written in "terms of speech, not speakers" and "offers no foothold for excluding any category of any category of speaker." In other words, they claimed that there is no basis in the Constitution (or English common law, as Scalia pointed out) for denying any corporation—or any association of persons—the First Amendment right to free speech. This gives corporations the same rights as persons in virtue of being an association of persons. Putting aside the question of whether BCRA expressed "the common sense of the American people," as Stevens opined, we still must question the claim made by Kennedy, Roberts, Alito, Scalia, and Thomas about associations of persons—say in corporate form—retaining the right to free speech. If the First Amendment does not admit or distinguish between categories of speaker and we agree that freedom of speech should be respected irrespective of the identity of the speaker, isn't the majority opinion self-evident and irrefutable?

Free Speech and Corporate Personhood:
The First Amendment says:

"Congress shall make no law respecting an establishment of religion, or prohibiting the free exercise thereof; or abridging the freedom of speech, or of the press; or the right of the people peacefully to assemble, and to petition the Government for a redress of grievances."

Clearly this applies to all political speech. If so, it should also apply to all forms of "electioneering communications," even blatant attack ads, and the onus is on the listeners or viewers to decide upon its merits for themselves. On such a view, propaganda and lies should be considered as protected speech alongside reasoned discourse and truth because it is not the job of government to tell us which is which, and it is for persons do decide for themselves how they receive speech. According to this view, it simply does not matter who speaks, what their motives are for speaking (i.e. whether they are honest or deceptive), and whether what they say is true or false. It is the speech that is protected.

Who are Citizens United? Citizens United is a non-profit corporation that funds, makes, and distributes political movies.[11] It is funded by Republicans.[12] It does not conceal this partisan political affiliation. On their website, Citizens United states that the purpose of the *Citizens United Political Victory Fund* (a PAC) is to collect donations to "support true conservative candidates running for federal office through direct candidate advocacy and contributions, based on our in-depth candidate research and surveys."[13] It also does not hide that Citizens United donates only to Republican candidates and has formed an "affiliate" called *The Presidential Coalition* to promote the election of Republican presidents, through "advocacy campaigns and candidate contributions." It also collects donations through the Citizens United Foundation, which is

"a 501(c)3 tax-exempt non-profit dedicated to informing the American people about public policy issues which relate to traditional American values: strong national defense, Constitutionally limited government, free market economics, belief in God and Judeo-Christian values, and the recognition of the family as the basic social unit of our society. CUF does not involve itself in any political campaigns, lobbying, or other activities."[14]

These "affiliates" cooperate with *Citizens United Productions* (CUP), which Citizens United describes as "the documentary film production and marketing arm of Citizens United. CUP has produced films with Newt and Callista Gingrich, Dick Morris, Congresswoman Michele Bachmann, Fred Thompson, and many other stars of the conservative movement. Many of our films have won film festival awards, including *Perfect Valor* (Best Documentary at the GI Film Festival) and *Ronald Reagan: Rendezvous with Destiny* (Remi Award at Houston Worldfest International Festival)."

It has also produced the following movies: *The Gift of Life with Governor Mike Huckabee*, an anti-abortion movie; *A City Upon a Hill: the Spirit of American Exceptionalism hosted by Newt and Callista Gingrich*, criticizing the Democratic Party and liberals for betraying "American exceptionalism"; *Battle for America with Dick Norris*, criticizing Barack Obama's presidency; *Fire from the Heartland: the Awakening of the Conservative Woman*, celebrating Republican politicians such as Sarah Palin and Michelle Bachmann as epitomizing strong conservative women defending American values from liberalism; *America at Risk: the War with No Name hosted by Newt and Callista Gingrich*, about how the Obama Administration is losing the war against Islamic jihadists and risking the destruction of America; *Nine Days that Changed the World hosted by Newt and Callista Gingrich*, about how Pope John Paul II and religious faith brought down the Soviet Bloc in Eastern Europe and, ultimately, the Soviet Union; *Generation Zero* about how the collapse of the financial sector in 2008 was not a failure of capitalism, but the result of a cultural failure evident in "the narcissism of the 1960s that spread like a virus into the self-indulgent 90s"; *Rediscovering God in America hosted by Newt and Callista Gingrich, volumes one and two* about how America was founded as a Christian country and Christianity has been the source of "American exceptionalism" throughout its history; *We Have the Power: Making America Energy Independent hosted by Newt and Callista Gingrich*, about how "the Left" and "environmentalists" have prevented American "energy independence" by imposing taxes on American oil companies, blocking drilling in ANWR, and opposing the building of new hydroelectric dams and nuclear reactors; *Blocking "The Path to 9/11": Anatomy of a Smear* on how the Clintons and some high ranking members of the Democratic Party conspired with ABC to censor an ABC "docudrama" *The Path to 9/11* that blamed the Clinton Administration for the September 11th 2001 attack on the World Trade Center;[15] *Broken Promises: The United Nations at 60* about the incompetence and impotence of the United Nations; *Hype: the Obama Effect* about the love affair between Barack Obama and "the liberal media"; *ACLU: At War With America*, about how liberals in the ACLU are "un-American haters of American values and traditions"; *Border War: The Battle Over Illegal Immigration*—the story of the struggle on the border to fend off the impending threat to America from an invasion of hordes of poor and angry Mexicans, along with organized criminal gangs and cartels, because "the right just want cheap labor, and the left just want cheap votes." And, predictably, *Celcius 41:11—The Temperature At Which The Brain Dies—The Truth Behind the Lies of Fahrenheit 9/11,* about why Michael Moore's movie *Fahrenheit 9/11* was propaganda and anyone who believes a word of it is brain dead.

Clearly all of these movies are examples of partisan political propaganda in favor of the GOP and against the Democrats. Whether donating to Citizens United constitutes an "independent expenditure" is open to question, and, arguably, SCOTUS should have heard testimony on this question, and it is also questionable whether Citizen United's claim that it does "not involve itself in any political campaigns" is true or not, and both of these questions should have formed the basis for deciding whether did the FEC acted fairly and consistently. Was *Hillary: The Movie* electioneering communication in a way that ads for Michael Moore's movie *Fahrenheit 9/11* were not? Was *Fahrenheit 9/11* also electioneering communication? The FEC said that it was not. This was a questionable and contestable decision, against which Citizens United had a legitimate right of appeal, given that Michael Moore used several well-known propaganda techniques juxtaposition, including the juxtaposition of images and narrative, suggestion, and the interplay between fact and speculation, sometimes asserted as fact, to invoke an emotional response against Bush, Cheney, and the rest of the Bush Administration, along with Halliburton, the Carlyle Group, and Fox News. These juxtapositions were also apparent in the ads for *Fahrenheit 9/11*, which did indeed mention a candidate—the incumbent president and vice-president—by name in the run up to the election. While stopping short of actually stating that the Bush Administration planned the attack on the World Trade Center, it is clearly suggested in the movie that Bush *et al*. took full advantage of this event to perpetrate a very profitable war against Iraq, for themselves and their financial backers in Saudi Arabia, Halliburton, the Carlyle Group, and News Corporation—with the complicity and help of Congress and the rest of corporate media—regardless of the consequences for Americans and the people of Iraq, and let the real planners in Saudi Arabia get away with it. It is apparent in *Fahrenheit 9/11* that Michael Moore did not consider Bush fit for re-election; he even made it quite clear that he did not consider Bush to have been elected in the first place. It simply does not matter whether the claims made in this movie are true or false, given that the purpose of the movie was one of informing the audience, ads aired during the run-up to the election were "electioneering communications," given that they could persuade undecided voters against Bush if they saw the movie before the election. Citizens United were right to demand that the FEC enforce BCRA. The FEC refusal was arbitrary. *Fahrenheit 9/11* is just as much an example of propaganda and electioneering communication as *Hillary: The Movie*.

What of *Hillary: The Movie*? Appealing to little more than speculation and innuendo, juxtaposed with carefully edited footage and narrative, this movie portrays Hillary Clinton as a sinister and calculating character who has managed to take cover behind her husband and "the liberal media" to avoid scrutiny, tough questions, and any investigation into possible corruption. Is this movie an example of propaganda? Even if the implications asserted by this movie were true, the movie does not show any evidence for them, and is more geared toward evoking an emotion of suspicion of Hillary Clinton. The use of proof by suspicion or innuendo rather than facts is one of the main hallmarks of propaganda. The aim is to bypass reasoning and appeal directly to emotions and prejudices. The reinforcement of prejudices is another hallmark of propaganda. The FEC was correct in considering this movie to be an example of "electioneering communication,"—given that it mentioned a candidate by name and could influence undecided delegates and voters—even if we consider this ruling to be inconsistent with the FEC ruling on Michael Moore's *Fahrenheit 9/11*, and, arguably, Citizens United was fully aware of this and made *Hillary* and timed its showing with the explicit purpose of exposing the FEC's inconsistency and forcing a challenge in the courts. The FEC took the bait.

However, having said all that, the SCOTUS majority did make it clear that it is speech that is protected by the First Amendment. It is also not at all evident that the "undecided" proportion of the electorate who paid to watch it on DirecTV; and negatively changed their view about Hillary Clinton as a result, would have influenced the actual outcome of the primary. Viewers could have just as likely decided that it was propaganda and biased. It is certainly arguable that the FEC block on showing *Hillary: The Movie* the night before the Democratic primary gave it much higher profile and far greater impact on the political process than it would have had the FEC had simply allowed it to be shown. Even if we consider Citizen United's *Hillary: The Movie* to be an example of nothing more than propaganda, which arguably it is (along with Michael Moore's *Fahrenheit 911*), it should still be protected under the First Amendment as an example of political speech. So, if taken at face value, it does not matter who the speaker is because the First Amendment protects the speech itself, and it does not matter what the intentions of the speaker are as the content of the speech is protected. It does not matter if "the speaker" is a corporation, union, or person, and it does not matter is the speech is deemed propaganda, one-sided, or a flat out lie. It is not for the FEC or Congress to decide who can speak, and whether their speech is true or false, educational or deceptive, or information or propaganda. That would be censorship. People must make those decisions for themselves. It is an individual or natural right of persons. If we agree about this, it is clearly the case that BCRA and the FEC did unconstitutionally muzzle the free speech of the group of people collectively known as Citizens United, regardless of who paid for their movie. The restrictions on when electioneering communications could be shown were violations of the First Amendment. Arguably, laws like DCRA unfairly benefits incumbents, given that they are already known to the electorate by name but their record may not.[16] It is easier to be re-elected if the opposition has no voice or forum in which to state its name and reasons for opposition. It is so much easier to be re-elected when critics are silenced or marginalized. Perhaps Justice Kennedy was correct when he suggested that BCRA was passed just to protect incumbents and gain "a governmental foothold on the slippery slope towards censoring newspapers and Internet bloggers."

It is for this reason that otherwise disparate groups such as the Commission on Federal Ethics Law and the American Civil Liberties Union came together to celebrate this ruling as one of defending the First Amendment and freedom of speech.[17] A spokesman for Citizens United put it this way:

"Today's U.S. Supreme Court decision allowing Citizens United to air its documentary films and advertisements is a tremendous victory, not only for Citizens United but for every American who desires to participate in the political process."

At a first glance, this seems to be a cut-and-dry case. A healthy democracy should allow anyone or any group—in whatever form—an opportunity to share opinions and criticisms with their fellow citizens. It is up to each member of the electorate to educate themselves and decide what they deem relevant or true, lies and falsehoods, information or propaganda. It is not the job of the government to do this for people. It should not matter who made or paid for a pay-for-view documentary or attack ad, such as *Hillary: The Movie*. If people wish to pay to watch it on DirecTV then government interference is censorship and in violation of the First Amendment. But, does this ruling really represent "a victory for every American who desires to participate in the political process"? Are more or less Americans able to participate in the political process as a result of this ruling? Why should we believe Congress's stated intention to protect the integrity of the electoral process? How do limits on electioneering communication protect the integrity of the electoral process? From what? Why does it matter whether corporations buy millions of dollars of political advertising?

Firstly, we need to ask whether a non-profit corporation like Citizens United has First Amendment rights. Secondly, we need to ask whether the government does have a compelling interest in restricting propaganda before an election to protect the integrity of the election from political corruption. Scratch the surface of the Citizen United ruling and we see how the ruling of the SCOTUS majority presupposed the legal fiction of *corporate personhood* and was judicial activism made on ideological rather than constitutional grounds. It is on that basis that Citizens United v FEC should be overturned.

Corporate personhood was implied when Roberts *et al.* asserted,

"The rule that political speech cannot be limited based on a speaker's wealth is a necessary consequence of the premise that the First Amendment generally prohibits the suppression of political speech based on the speaker's identity."

He assumed that the donation of shareholders' money by managers or directors is a form of political speech and the corporation is a speaker, and the issue advocacy ads and electioneering communications paid for by corporate money are speech. From this perspective, corporations are merely just another form of an association of persons, for which their collective right to free speech should be protected.

However, Roberts *et al.* ignored two legal facts that make corporations unlike persons: (1) The SCOTUS majority have ignored the fact that *a corporation is property—a legal entity defined by state law—designed to make money for shareholders*, aside from any political or moral concerns. Directors and managers of corporations are obliged *by law* to maximize profits for their shareholders, over and above any other concern or priority.[18] Unlike persons, corporations cannot have a wide range of interests and concerns. (2) *Limited liability*, which is a legal protection that limits the liability of shareholders only to risk their initial investment and protects them from any debts incurred while they were in corporate form, *is not afforded by law to individuals*. Persons acting in corporate form have a legal status that is not granted to persons acting alone. Applying the Fourteenth Amendment equal protection clause—thereby granting corporations First Amendment rights—ignores the inequality that already exists in law between corporations and persons. Corporations are not just people, they are also people with special legal rights as a result of associating in corporate form. This legal difference discredits the assumed soundness of the majority presumption of corporate personhood and that this case was a First Amendment issue.

The assertion that corporations—as collective associations of persons—retain the First Amendment rights of persons as individuals brushes aside the fact that persons who associate in corporate form also retain their right to free speech as individuals, regardless of whether they are associated in corporate form or not. This assertion allows double-dipping, so to speak. Contrary to the SCOTUS majority's opinion, people do not lose the right to free speech if the directors of a corporation they have stock in were not allowed to spend shareholders' money to pay for the production and airing of political campaign ads during the run-up to primaries and elections; just as people do not lose their right to free speech if corporations or unions of any kind cannot donate hard money to political candidates. As individuals, people remain free to donate to political candidates, political parties, PACS, and non-profit organizations like Citizens United. This was not changed by BCRA. Even if each and every dollar spent on a political campaign for election could be traced back to an individual person, and any limits on donations applied equally to all citizens, everyone would be equal under the law and receive equal protection from the law, including the protection of the right to free speech. Money should only be considered as speech when it is given directly by individuals for speech, and the government does have a compelling interest in tracking donations and expenditures as only members of the electorate, citizens, should be allowed to donate to political campaigns and influence elections. Violations to this restriction could be considered as racketeering, embezzlement, and corruption, as well as leaving elections open to foreign influences, from investors, governments, and multi-national corporations.

It is also the case that, when corporations make donations to non-profits to make and distribute electioneering communications and issue advocacy ads, corporate directors or managers are using *other people's money* to support or oppose candidates or issues, without informing those people and gaining their consent. *Shareholder money is spent without the consent of the shareholders*, apart from their tacit consent to allow directors decision-making power regarding the best way to maximize profits. The majority's reliance on an overly simplistic definition of a corporation as "a form of association of persons" (as if it were no different from a town hall meeting or a group of friends) ignores the hierarchical and complex internal organization of corporate governance. In most corporations, shareholder governance is quite limited.[19] Regardless of the assertions of Roberts *et al.*, BCRA did not remove the right of people to exercise free speech when they associate in corporate form. Shareholders still retain their right as an individual to donate money to any advocacy group, church, foundation, or charity, and PACs. This right was not taken away from shareholders by BCRA. Nor was their right to free speech curtailed during the run-up to primaries and elections. They could talk to anyone who will listen about any candidate they wish and say anything they want about that candidate, any time they wish to say it. Individuals still remain free to volunteer, join political associations and engage in independent expenditures. However it is dressed up, the corporate decision-making process about how to maximize profits does not as readily equate with the free speech of shareholders as the SCOTUS majority would assert. It is more akin to a right of spending, which is not a constitutional right. The only right that BCRA took away was the legal right of people to act on behalf of a corporation or unions to use shareholder or members' money to purchase ad space from media corporations, and broadcast advocacy ads and electioneering communications during a primary or election and disseminate advocacy ads for or against a political candidate or issue in the run up to that election or primary.

But why should investors' consent matter? As an investor, I may well consider an arms manufacturer with good defense contracts to be a sound investment. Obviously it is in my interest as an investor that the government awards contracts to the arms manufacturer, thereby increasing profits and the value of my investment. However, it does not follow from this that I would *necessarily* support pro-war candidates and oppose anti-war candidates in any election simply because this would increase the short-term return on my investment in an arms manufacturer if America was involved in another war. My interests in peace and diplomacy, alongside a long-term view of the economic viability of stable international relations between countries, may well trump any short-term returns war might bring. Whether I make any such value judgment is something that is independent from and over-and-above any evaluation of the short-term financial return on my investments. I may well also oppose war for moral or religious reasons, regardless of whatever financial gains it may bring my way, while respecting my nation's right to self-defense and having a large and well-equipped military. In this case, I would necessarily not want my money to fund electioneering communications for a candidate that called for a new war, and may well prefer candidates who advocate diplomacy. As investors, people may well seek a good rate of return on their investment, but as citizens they may well be appalled by political corruption and seek to elect a politician who will serve the public good rather than his or her own self-interest. Similarly, I may well respect a particular candidate's grasp of business and sound economics, but might find their rhetoric on immigrants or minority groups appalling and bigoted. There can be a contradiction between short-term economic interests and enduring political or moral values that cannot be resolved simply by assuming that appealing to the former implies consent regarding whatever is said in the name of the latter. The resolution of that contradiction is itself a political problem that should be decided through the political process by the electorate, without allowing that process to be dominated only by the short-term economic interests of corporations. In the end, the electorate may decide that short-term economic interests (more money, jobs, and lower prices) should trump long-term political interests, but that decision is for the electorate to decide. The political process should not be rigged in advance for only short-term economic interests to be represented.

The SCOTUS majority ruling does exactly this: it rigs the election process in advance to allow corporate money to dominate it. The SCOTUS majority have simply assumed corporate spending on electioneering communications is nothing other than political speech, regardless of whether shareholders give their consent. Yet there is no legal basis for the identification of a person's consent to pool their money with the investments of others in a corporate form for economic reasons *with* their consent to have their money used to support a political issue or candidate. Strictly speaking, speech can only be said to be free if it is independent from constraint or coercion, and it is said with the consent of the speaker. It always remains possible that a corporate director can support a political candidate that individual investors might strongly oppose for public office. It seems a little perverse to describe someone else using shareholders' money in a way that the shareholders would not consent to as an example of shareholders exercising the right to free speech by having their own money spent for them. Yet, perversity notwithstanding, under the umbrella of defending the First Amendment, the majority dismissed as irrelevant any suggestion that there is a requirement that shareholders should consent to the content of the "speech" made on their behalf, as, apparently, their right to free speech is exercised when their money is spent regardless of whatever their own political views so happen to be and whatever is said on their behalf. Roberts *et al.* opined,

"It is irrelevant for purposes of the First Amendment that corporate ideas may 'have little or no correlation with the public support for the corporation's political ideas.' All speakers, including individuals and the media, use money amassed from the economic marketplace to fund their speech. The First Amendment protects the resulting speech, even if it was enabled by economic interactions with persons or entities who disagree with the speaker's ideas."

Yet, contrary to the SCOTUS majority assertion, corporations do not have political ideas. People have political ideas. There is no reason to suppose that people who associate as a corporation share unanimously or even as a majority the same political ideas. Human associations are complex and dynamic. It is unreasonable to assume that members of an association will always unanimously agree on moral and political matters that do not pertain to their economic reason for associating in the form of a corporation. People may well think that Comcast is a great business, but it does not follow from this that they will agree with each other on issues that don't relate to business. Economic and commercial considerations are an important part of human existence, but they are not the only part. For human beings, unlike corporations, there are important moral and social considerations too. We have families, neighbors, friends, communities, and lives, unlike corporations. We live in a social and natural environment, needing clean air, water, and nourishing food, enjoying and developing healthy human relations and cultural experiences. We feel pain, hope, fear, anger, love, and, unlike corporations, we die. Many human beings view the natural world as something worthy of respect, wonder, and awe—responses a corporation cannot have—and for some human beings, we feel a sense of divine origin—a Creator, Nature's God, who bestows these rights upon human beings, declared self-evident by Thomas Jefferson in *The Declaration of Independence*. This notion of natural rights belonging to persons is fundamental to the very idea of rights of the Constitution and the Bill of Rights. We are not a creation of state law, unlike corporations. Corporations are legal constructs that do not have inalienable, natural or God-given rights. Corporations are property, nothing more. The SCOTUS majority have over-simplified and reduced human psychology and politics to the satisfaction of economic imperatives and short-term financial interests. They dismissed any other value as irrelevant. *Only* money is speech.

Even the political speech of shareholders is silenced by the SCOTUS majority's ruling. Speech is apparently not what people say, but it is what is said on their behalf. Roberts's concern was not with protecting the political speech of individual persons, but only the right of corporations to spend money to influence elections. On one side the right to free speech of the persons who have associated in corporate form is to be protected, while on the other it does not matter even if individuals disagree with what is said using their money. This ruling was not about protecting individual rights at all. It was judicial activism to allow corporations and other moneyed interests to dominate the political process by preventing Congress from having any authority to legislate and regulate that process. Regardless of their pretensions to stick to the Constitution, for Roberts *et al.*, they granted corporations rights *over and above* the association of persons that form those corporations, insofar as it does not matter what the shareholders' own political choices might so happen to be, and they ultimately undermined the sovereignty of the people and their elected legislature. Profits are paramount, and however corporate directors deem investors' money to be best spent to increase profits has been treated as a right by the SCOTUS ruling, which overrides all other considerations even if that involves attempting to influence elections by choreographed media blitzes of cross-platform attack ads slandering political candidates, without those candidates having any right of reply, in the run-up to primaries and elections. Roberts *et al.* have a point in that the First Amendment pertains to the speech itself and not who says it, but it does not follow from this point that people when acting on behalf of other people associated in corporate form have any constitutional right to purchase speech to influence elections.

By assuming that spending money on speech is synonymous with speech, Roberts *et al.* have allowed an economic form of organization to use revenue generated through its economic activities to insert money into the political process, and therefore this case is really about the property rights of corporations to spend shareholders' money, as a business expense, to influence the political organization of everyone else, regardless of whether the insertion of money on elections would inevitably corrupt the political process. Roberts *et al.* refused to hear any testimony on the government's compelling interest in preventing this from happening, and therefore SCOTUS have placed the property rights of corporations over and above the constitutional rights of everyone else. Even if all the shareholders (or union members) were in agreement about how their collective money should be spent on elections, in addition to their own individual contributions, this still does not override the compelling interest of the government and the people to protect the integrity of the political process and limit expenditure during elections. The only freedom at stake here is the freedom of the people, as citizens, to govern their own affairs in accordance to a much wider range of values and concerns than only that of maximizing the next quarterly profits and share dividends.

Once we recognize that the SCOTUS majority turned this case into a case about money, we can see that Citizens United vs. FEC is really a property dispute case about whether the government, acting on behalf of the people, has a constitutional right to limit how corporate managers and directors spend other peoples' money on electioneering communications, or whether the First Amendment protects the right of corporate managers to spend shareholders' money on whatever advertisements they deem will benefit the corporation's bottom-line. However, was SCOTUS the best venue for this property dispute? Corporations are not mentioned in the Constitution. The enumerated rights belong to individual persons, not corporations. It is often claimed that personhood was granted to corporations under the equal protection clause of the

Fourteenth Amendment by SCOTUS in *Santa Clara County v Southern Pacific Railroad*, 1886. This is an error. In fact, SCOTUS refused to rule on this case as a Fourteenth Amendment issue and instead ruled that the case narrowly pertained to whether the fences alongside railroad tracks could be included by the State of California as taxable property. The court ruled that they could not be. It did not rule on any constitutional questions, yet the court clerk J.C. Bancroft Davis wrote down the court's opinion of the constitutional issue, as the summary of the court's ruling—the heading note—even though the court had refused to rule on that issue. This "clerical error" has been mistakenly been taken as legal precedence for corporate personhood by people who only read the heading note and not the actual ruling. This heading note reads as follows:

"The court does not wish to hear argument on the question whether the provision in the Fourteenth Amendment to the Constitution, which forbids a State to deny to any person within its jurisdiction the equal protection of the laws, applies to these corporations. We are all of the opinion that it does."

The legal fiction of corporate personhood actually dates back to 1819 in the case of *Dartmouth College v Woodward* when SCOTUS ruled that a corporation, as an association of persons, should be considered as a single person for purposes of making a contract, owning property, and conducting business.

Hence by making it a property dispute, Citizens United became a person with free speech. It was only under the spell of the legal fiction of corporate personhood that SCOTUS could consider the First Amendment as being applicable in Citizen United's case. As court precedent shows, the Bill of Rights trumps the Articles, especially in the case of political speech, and corporate personhood was implicit in the translation through association of the individual's right to free speech to the collected right to free speech. The notion of corporate personhood is operational at least in the sense that the corporation *represents* the collective personhood of its shareholders, each of whom has a right to free speech, but without any of the responsibilities and liabilities that individual persons have, including citizenship requirements to vote, and regardless of their own individual political opinions. Clerical errors and the establishment of personhood status for contractual purposes aside, there is not any necessary and sufficient reason—certainly not one based on the Constitution—why the First Amendment should apply to corporate spending whatsoever on issue advocacy ads or electioneering communications. BCRA did not even prohibit such spending. It simply restricted it, along with everyone else's spending. Individuals were also still able to donate to PACs and directly to non-profits like Citizens United.

Don't people have a constitutional right to the use of their property? Yes, but this is not an absolute right, and the Constitution limits how people use their property if that use has consequences for other people, and it also gives Congress and state legislatures the authority to levy taxes, thereby taking a proportion of people's property to pay for defense, law enforcement, and to promote the General Welfare. The Constitution places everyone equal under the law. This is why we have laws to protect other people by placing limits on our actions, which in turn protects each of us from other people's actions. This is the implicit social contract that legitimates the whole concept of law, equality under the law, and the rights enumerated in the Bill of Rights. The Constitution does not grant people any absolute right over their property, but affords some limited protections and property rights as granted to them by law. Property rights are legal constructs, as defined by the legislatures. Congress already has the authority to prevent or limit the ability of people to use or refuse to use their property in a way that has consequences for other people. The Constitution gives Congress the authority to tax in Article I (and the Sixteenth Amendment) and the Fifth Amendment empowers the government to take private property "for public use," providing that "just compensation" is paid. Rightly or wrongly, the Constitution grants the government the authority to use other people's property in ways that they themselves would not use it if left to their own devices. The Constitution also grants the government the authority to protect the political process, the stability of the union, and the General Welfare of the states and people. This constitutional obligation of government (and among those who have sworn an oath to protect the Constitution) provides the government with a compelling interest to legislate and regulate elections to product the integrity of the whole political process and the legitimacy of the government. Of course First Amendment protections must prohibit the government from censoring speech, and therefore SCOTUS did have a point about the unconstitutionality of restricting electioneering communications in the run up to primaries and elections, but this does not equate to any imaginary right to spend unlimited amounts of money on electioneering communications, in the same way that concerns for the public good overrides the First Amendment in cases involving sedition, use of provocation or "fighting words," endangering others (such as shouting "Fire!" in a crowded theater), or obscenity.[20]

In fact, the Constitution explicitly grants state legislatures and Congress jurisdiction over elections. This is specified in Article I, Section 4:

"The Times, Places and Manner of holding Elections for Senators and Representatives, shall be prescribed in each State by the Legislature thereof; but the Congress may at any time by Law make or alter such Regulations, except as to the Place of Chusing Senators."

And Article III, section 2:

"the Supreme Court shall have appellate jurisdiction, both as to law and fact, *with such exceptions, and under such regulations as the Congress shall make.*"

This grants both state legislatures and Congress the authority to declare that campaign finance reforms, such as laws like BCRA, are exceptions to the jurisdiction of SCOTUS and therefore the manner under which elections are conducted are a matter for state legislatures and Congress to decide, not SCOTUS.

Once we acknowledge that both public interest in the integrity of the electoral process and the Constitution grants Congress jurisdiction over elections, thereby giving the government a compelling interest in protecting the integrity of the political process, we should argue that SCOTUS's considerations should have been limited to the question of whether BCRA had been legally applied by the FEC to Citizens United, with the main concern being whether this was a legal block or a case of overreach or arbitrariness. Steven's dissent was right. The SCOTUS majority engaged in judicial activism by changing the case so they could change the law. This was inconsistent with precedent. After *Burroughs v United States*, 1934 and *the United States v Classic*, 1941, the Supreme Court upheld the 1910 Federal Corrupt Practices Act, until it was repealed by FECA. For over a century, the Supreme Court has recognized that Congress does have the constitutional authority to prevent corruption and the integrity of the political process, especially during elections, and has left it to Congress to decide how best to achieve this. By overturning precedence, Roberts *et al.* have undermined Congress's authority to establish legislative checks and balances and to regulate the electoral process. The SCOTUS majority have undermined the Constitution and the separation of powers. It is for this reason that some commentators have claimed that the equation of money with speech is the main issue, and that Congress could appeal to Articles I and III to challenge the constitutionality of the Supreme Court's ruling, without needing to address corporate personhood in a constitutional amendment.[21]

Corruption:

What is the rationale behind limits to expenditures? Clearly advocates of limits believe that money buys more media time and reach, and political advertising influences the electorate, so limits to expenditures prevents one wealthy group or groups from dominating media campaigns. Roberts *et al.* looked at advocacy issue ads in isolation and thereby argued abstractly that they could as equally harm as benefit a candidate. They took *Hillary: The Movie* in isolation and asserted that "independent expenditures" on this one movie could not unduly influence or corrupt politicians or give the appearance of doing so. Therefore, according to the SCOTUS majority, government had no compelling interest in preventing this or any other movie from being shown in the run-up to a primary, or even in limiting how much money can be spent on electioneering communications. If the prevention of corruption or the appearance of corruption, either of which undermines the political process, is not a compelling interest for the government, the majority opinion is that BCRA restrictions on spending or when electioneering communications can be aired was not narrowly tailored and constituted governmental overreach. While this is true of any advertisement taken in isolation, as it could be true of anything at all, what the majority ignored was the way that these kinds of electioneering communications can be coordinated as part of an overall media strategy to dominate political speech and silence all other speakers. Not only would the SCOTUS majority decision entail overturning city ordinances against loud music and noise pollution, as violations of the First Amendment, given that we cannot say that any loud music taken in isolation is noise pollution or enjoyable music, Robert's *et al.* were pretty much saying that because we cannot say that any one particular advertisement for Hershey's chocolate influenced a child to want Hershey's chocolate, if that ad is taken in isolation, there is no reason to believe that advertising chocolate makes children wants chocolate at all, and therefore the government has no compelling interest in preventing chocolate advertisements in schools or even not allowing advertisers to target children with specific products, say tobacco, alcohol, or contraceptives. By analogy with the SCOTUS majority ruling, it should be a First Amendment violation for the government to prohibit the showing of advertisements for cigarettes, cocktail mixers, and adult entertainment on children's television channels or during daytime television hours. If we insisted on treating each and every advertisement in isolation, there is no evidence that any advertisement for cigarettes ever encouraged anybody to want to smoke one, and there would seem little point in advertising at all. Madison Avenue might as well close its doors.

The SCOTUS majority ruling also ignored the problem of corruption and revolving-door politics. They ignored that electioneering communications are expensive and the ability of moneyed interests to dominate electioneering communications can influence incumbents and candidates to satisfy those moneyed interests once the election is over. They ignored the implicit *quid pro quo* of donations and expenditures from economic organizations. Corporations spend money on electioneering communications because directors and managers believe it will have an effect on the outcome of the election. This is the same reason why people donate to campaigns. Money is needed to pay to get the message out and persuade other people to vote for their preferred candidate, or at least not vote for the other guy. This ruling has been a boon to PACs and non-profit advocacy organizations—leading the creation of Super PACs and multi-billion dollar spending on elections. During the run up to the 2012 presidential election we saw a massive amount of corporate money flow into PACs and Super PACs to make and broadcast issue advocacy ads and electioneering communications (or arrange for favorable editorials in the newspapers, blogs, and social media sound-bites.) Over $2 billion dollars was spent on the 2012 presidential election campaigns, with both candidates spending about the same amount. Corporations spent huge amounts of money on the election campaigns of both the incumbent president Barack Obama and the GOP candidate Mitt Romney, as well as for elections to Congress and state legislatures, and local and city offices. If money is speech, and each dollar a unit of speech, then can we calculate how much influence a single dollar had on the outcome of the election? Can we assume that the candidates who outspend their opponents will always win? Taking the 2012 election as an example, both candidates raised about the same amount of money, and, if anything, Romney raised slightly more than Obama, yet Obama won by a clear majority. Was there an incumbency factor? How much more money would Romney have needed to spend to change the result?

Even if we assume shareholder consent with how their money is spent on elections, we can hardly consider political campaign spending to be a way of maximizing profits unless there is a reasonable expectation of a return on that expenditure in the form of favorable legislation or government contracts—*quid pro quo*. Directors and managers would be acting illegally and in bad faith with the shareholders if this *quid pro quo* was not implicit in the donation or expenditure. It would be embezzlement. Obviously corporations can gain or lose profits as a result of government policies and regulations; hence lobbyists exist. Corruption is inevitable if corporations and big business are allowed unlimited expenditure on electioneering communications and issue advocacy ads. The corporate justification for spending shareholders' money on election campaigns is that one candidate will increase the corporation's business and profits, or another candidate will hinder and decrease them. It comes down to the bottom line. Corporations do not donate money out of a spirit of charity but purely out of a concern with their business and its profits, as the law compels them. If politicians do not play the *quid pro quo* game, they will find themselves without donors when it comes around to the next election. If a politician or any elected official does not give corporate lobbyists what they want, corporations can pay to flood the airwaves, cable TV, and satellite radio and TV with attack ads against him or her and support his or her opponents instead. Once politicians are beholden to corporate donors for election and re-election, corporations then act as gate-keepers for nomination and election to federal office. If politicians are beholden to corporate sponsors and corporate media—if they hope to be re-elected—this state of affairs clearly tends towards corruption and cronyism. This clearly not only threatens the integrity of the political process and elections by bombarding media with propaganda, and shutting out all other voices, but it effectively leaves corporations and their lobbyists to write the laws of the land, gain lucrative government contracts, and deduct their lobbying and political expenditures from their taxes. When this happens, representative democracy becomes a plutocracy, wherein moneyed interests control all the institutions of government and media, and, once that happens, the rate of transformation from a democratic republic into a corporate state accelerates, and the electorate are increasingly limited to choosing between one of two pro-corporate interest candidates.

As a result, any political system that allows large sums of money to be donated for campaign expenditures from commercial and economic interests opens the door to corruption and cronyism. The SCOTUS majority have legalized the corruption of the political process, and seriously tied the hands of Congress in writing legislation to prevent corruption and the appearance of corruption. Cronyism and corruption are the inevitable consequence of a political culture of *quid pro quo* if money is taken to be speech and unlimited corporate spending on political propaganda is permissible. The SCOTUS ruling has not only legalized corruption, but makes it a necessary component of both corporate operations and the political process, thereby necessitating corruption as a fundamental aspect of doing business and politics. The SCOTUS majority have normalized corruption and cronyism by making them inevitable aspects of being successful within commerce and the political process.

The SCOTUS majority did not rest their judicial activism at insisting that corporations should be allowed to dominate federal elections. The Montana Supreme Court, in *Western Tradition Partnership, Inc. v Attorney General of Montana*, 2011, upheld the State's Corrupt Practices Law limiting corporate contributions, given the history of corporate interference in Montana state elections. In June 2012, despite Justices Ginsburg and Breyer's statement that SCOTUS should reconsider "whether, in light of the huge sums of money currently deployed to buy candidate's allegiance, Citizens United should continue to hold sway," Roberts *et al.* summarily reversed the Montana Supreme Court's ruling. Ignoring the Montana Supreme Court's appeal to the history of corruption and corporate interference in elections in the state of Montana, as well as its arguments for why Citizens United did not apply to this case, the SCOTUS majority rejected the Montana Supreme Court arguments as being either already rejected in Citizens United, or failing to meaningfully distinguish the Western Tradition case from it. They asserted that states cannot bar corporate expenditures in state elections.

This pro-corporate bias was even more apparent in the SCOTUS majority ruling in the consolidated cases *Arizona Free Enterprise Club's Freedom Club PAC v Bennett*, 2011, and *McComish v Bennett*, 2011, when Roberts *et al.* ruled that the Arizona state law violated the First Amendment by providing public funds to candidates who were outspent by private donations and expenditures. The SCOTUS majority argued that the state legislature's efforts to "level the playing field" were unconstitutional because they disincentivized private fundraising and spending, thereby placing a burden on the political speech of private contributors. Perversely, Roberts *et al.* asserted that any method of public financing that attracts candidates who would otherwise be vastly outspent violated the First Amendment rights of privately funded candidates who could outspend them. This is another example of judicial activism. Not only does this ruling continue to equate money with speech, but it grants candidates for public office with a constitutional right to receive and spend more money from private donations than they could from public funds, and, somewhat perversely, asserts that any law that offers an attractive system of public financing violates this right in virtue of being attractive. States are only allowed to subsidize political campaigns and expenditures if public funding methods act as an alternative to private financing that do not compete with it. In other words, any system of public funding that competes with corporate funding is unconstitutional in virtue of competing, and candidates or parties that refuse corporate money and accept public funding instead must be at a funding disadvantage by law.

The Roberts majority were able to deliver the coup de grace to legislative efforts to limit corporate money in elections on April 2, 2014, when SCOTUS ruled in *McCutcheon v. FEC*, by a vote of 5-4, that aggregate limits on the amount an individual may contribute during a two-year period to all federal candidates, parties and political action committees combined, were unconstitutional under the First Amendment. BCRA's limits on the amounts that individuals may contribute to federal candidates and other political committees were overturned. Roberts wrote,

"The right to participate in democracy through political contributions is protected by the First Amendment, but that right is not absolute. Our cases have held that Congress may regulate campaign contributions to protect against corruption or the appearance of corruption… Congress may target only a specific type of corruption—'*quid pro quo*' corruption… Spending large sums of money in connection with elections, but not in connection with an effort to control the exercise of an officeholder's official duties, does not give rise to *quid pro quo* corruption. Nor does the possibility that an individual who spends large sums may garner 'influence over or access to' elected officials or political parties."

The SCOTUS majority ruled that

"the aggregate limits on contributions do not further the only governmental interest this Court accepted as legitimate in *Buckley*. They instead intrude without justification on a citizen's ability to exercise the most fundamental First Amendment activities."

And overturned the overall cap on individual contributions to federal candidate campaigns, PACs or party committees.

As the growing public backlash against the Citizens United ruling shows, the appearance of the revolving-door politics of corruption and cronyism has greatly undermined public faith in the American political process and elections. Given the compelling interest of Congress to avoid even the appearance of corruption, cronyism, and revolving-door politics, it has a compelling interest in setting down comprehensive laws on how it conducts elections including campaign spending limits and disclosure requirements. This has been understood by SCOTUS for the last 150 years. While it is reasonable for SCOTUS to hear and rule on challenges to any particular provisions or restrictions of any law like BCRA, it was a clear case of judicial activism for the Robert's majority to break with precedent and deny Congress the authority to legislate any expenditure limits or restrictions on electioneering communications. Regardless of its shortcomings, BCRA attempted to prevent primary and election campaigns from being dominated by people with access to the large sums of money, and therefore dominating access to mass media.

Propaganda:
How should the government deal with electioneering communications during the run up to primaries and elections if it is to both respect freedom of speech and the integrity of the electoral process? Why is it in a compelling interest of government to protect the electorate from propaganda? BCRA was quite narrowly tailored to place a limit on electioneering communication to prevent attack ads on any candidate for 30 days during the run-up to primaries and 60 days during the run-up elections. The idea behind this limitation was to give the candidate time for a right of reply to any accusations by running their own electioneering communications and issue advocacy ads. In a large country such as America, wherein constituents have little if any direct access to their representatives, mass media becomes the gatekeeper for election to federal office. Most people only know candidates by what they see on TV or online, hear on the radio, or read in the newspaper. Political speech is more often than not disseminated as sound-bites and slogans, without much in the way of follow-up questioning or fact-based analysis, running through increasingly rapid news cycles and interspersed with sponsored content and infomercials. Decades of psychological research and political

science conclude that people are irrationally swayed by the last opinions that they see or hear.[22] People need time to process the information they have received from media in order to come to an informed decision. If this research is true, it would mean that whoever could buy "the last word" would be at an unfair advantage, which would go to the highest bidder. It makes a significant difference whether people hear or see critical ads about a candidate a few times or dozens of times. Repetition does have an effect. Bombardment has a dramatic effect. It also makes a difference when the same message is broadcast or conveyed from seemingly independent sources. By funding PACs and non-profits, corporations can hide their support or opposition to candidates, and present the deception that viewers and listeners are seeing or hearing the same messages from different sources, giving it an illusionary appearance of corroboration and credibility.

SCOTUS ignored the problem of propaganda. Once electioneering communication is incorporated into a comprehensive strategy applied across diverse media sources to saturate the airwaves and print with propaganda, giving the appearance of independent corroboration and agreement, then it is clearly the case that attack ads do have a negative effect on candidates mentioned by name. The SCOTUS majority's ruling ignores that if associations can make accusations against a candidate, without any right to reply, then candidates are subjected to a barrage of attack ads as part of an orchestrated campaign against that candidate by a relatively small number of people who are able to purchase large amounts of airtime. These ads do not need to prove their factuality. They can slander or suggest via innuendo, and should be treated by the law in the same way that any libelous remark is treated.[23] Should propaganda be banned during election campaigns? Who is to say what is propaganda and what is political speech? Can we leave such decisions up to the FEC or Congress? My view is that we need to look at the problem at a deeper level than the SCOTUS majority did when considering such questions, and SCOTUS should have heard testimony before deciding on whether the government had a compelling interest in restricting electioneering communications and issue advocacy ads in the run up to primaries and elections, and whether BCRA was narrowly tailored to do that. Arguably BCRA attempted to prevent the kind of propaganda war that tends to favor the victory of whoever who can spend the most on the production and dissemination of electioneering communications and issue advocacy ads. Restrictions on spending frees candidates from the every escalating demands of fund-raising. Once we interpret the BCRA definition of the terms "issue advocacy ad" and "electioneering communications" as being code words for propaganda, we can see that the rationale behind BCRA was to protect people from being bombarded with political propaganda during the run up to primaries and elections, as well as to protect politicians from negative campaigns by advocacy groups, thereby turning election campaigns into a spending war. Reducing campaign expenditures does benefit incumbents, but it also benefits anyone wanting to run for federal office and challenge an incumbent.

If we acknowledge that political propaganda works, which is a relatively uncontentious claim (outside of the minds of the authors of the SCOTUS majority), and consider the amount of money spent on it, it is even more troubling for the integrity of the electoral process if the highest bidder comes in the form of an economic association such as a corporation, especially multi-national corporations, which may be beholden to foreign governments and investors. You don't need to be a registered voter or a citizen to donate or spend on an election via corporate expenditures. When the financial interests of shareholders are not necessarily the same as the political interests of the members of the electorate there is an inherent conflict of interest that can undermine the political process if corporations are allowed to dominate electioneering communications during political campaigns, leading to a government that does not act in the interests of the electorate. This not only means that foreign investors can gain influence in U.S. elections through subsidiaries and Super PACs, and by corporate expenditures paying to make and disseminate propaganda, it also means that the content of political speech and criticism during elections becomes narrowly selected to represent the interests of corporations rather than the electorate in general.

By isolating the movie *Hillary* from the rest of political culture, as if it exists "in splendid isolation," the majority ruling seems to rest on the somewhat naïve beliefs that political propaganda does not work and corporate money cannot corrupt or influence elected politicians through coordinated and choreographed expenditures through seemingly independent media sources, think-tanks, and non-profit corporations. Flying in the face of common sense and the results of psychological research and political science, Roberts *et al.* seem to be secure in their shared belief that should corruption or undue influence occur, the appearance of corruption or undue influence will not undermine public faith in the political process. Given that SCOTUS did not hear any testimony on the efficacy of political propaganda or whether Citizens United even qualified as being independent, or the effects of spending on the integrity of the political process, the majority ruling does seem at best to be a rather rash and foolish application of ideology, an example of judicial activism, and at worst the possible consequence of corruption and undue influence of corporate interests over particular supreme court justices.[24] After all, if political propaganda does not work, why do corporations want to spend all this money on advocacy ads and propaganda? Surely limits are just saving them from wasting their money! Is it really impossible to tell the difference between propaganda and free speech? Can you really call it free speech when you have to pay someone else to say it for you?

Arguably all political speech is propaganda. We know that propaganda works. This is why Citizens United v FEC is even an issue. But this issue reflects more than a need for campaign finance reform and limits to campaign spending. It gets to the heart of big moneyed corruption and the ownership of media. Through media control and manipulation, politicians and moneyed interests that have colluded in the corporate takeover of elections and all three branches of government. The first challenge is to get the money out of politics. This involves overturning the *Buckley vs. Valeo* equation of money with speech. But it more importantly involves the proportion of the electorate who don't have money to give their time and participation in the electoral process by informing themselves, helping in campaigns, canvasing and talking to their fellow citizens, and actually voting.[25]

Access to Media and the Political Process:
The SCOTUS majority ruling did raise an interesting and important problem. They argued that it is arbitrary to make a distinction between media corporations and any other corporation by allowing the former to editorialize and even make endorsements but censor the latter. Why should a media corporation have the right to disseminate propaganda, ignore or editorialize a candidate, or even tell downright lies during an election campaign, but this same right be denied to other corporations? How does one association of people get to have this right while another is denied it? After all, the owners of stock in media corporations can own stock in any kind of corporation, which in turn can legally own media corporations. Comcast, for example, owns NBC Universal Media (which operates NBC and Telemundo in all 50 states, and throughout Latin America) alongside radio stations, several broadcast and cable networks (including Adelphia Communications and the Westinghouse Group Cable), broadband Internet service providers, movie studios (including Universal Studios), and even theme parks (including Universal Studios Hollywood and Orlando). There is nothing to stop Comcast from acquiring newspapers and publishing houses. The Roberts majority have a point. It does seem arbitrary for media corporations to be granted First Amendment rights denied to other corporations, when those other corporations may well own media corporations. It seems that First Amendment rights should be granted to everyone, regardless of how they should so happen to associate.

There are three possible responses to this ruling. Either

(i) "The press" is a special category. The SCOTUS majority argued that it is inconsistent to treat media corporations as different from any other kind of corporation and therefore there cannot be any political speech restrictions placed on any kind of corporation. However, as well as ignoring that the First Amendment specifically includes the press as so protected, this argument is also flies in the face of SCOTUS precedent.[26] Historically, SCOTUS has had no difficulty in distinguishing between media corporations and other kinds of corporation. Even if we agree that it is unconstitutional to ban media corporations (or any media) from presenting political commentary about named candidates during primary and election campaigns, it is a non-sequitur to conclude that the right to political speech therefore belongs to all corporations because media corporations are the same as any other corporation. We might consider Fox News or MSNBC to be biased, and it is inevitable that all media is biased, but they still warrant special protection nevertheless. The First Amendment already establishes "the press" as a special case due to its value for protecting political speech and petitioning the government, and presumably to inform and educate the people about candidates for election to federal offices. To the extent that any media corporation can make a claim to be part of "the press," the First Amendment affords it special protection that it does not afford to the manufacturers of paper clips, beverages, or intercontinental ballistic missiles. The reason why we would consider it intolerable for the government to prevent Fox News or MSNBC from commenting on candidates during primaries or election campaigns is because (rightly or wrongly) we place these media corporations as valuable for learning about the candidates. It is for that reason that newspapers and publishers have been consistently included by the courts under the special category of "the press," affording journalists special rights and protections, and we hold "the press" to be essential for the political process and free speech, and to act as a watchdog and ensure the fair election of good candidates for public office. This is the case regardless of whether or not any particular media corporations are able to live up to that responsibility.

Or,

(ii) Corporate news media are not able to live up to their responsibility as "the press" and do not warrant special constitutional protections. News and opinion are sold in the same way as any other product. Informing the public is a service. Either laws like BCRA should have been applied equally to anyone when they are using the publicly-owned airwaves, or it violated the rights of everyone. We probably wouldn't want the FEC to be adjudicating statements of fact made during news broadcasts on corporate media, deciding which segment is classified as "news" or "editorial commentary," or classified as "issue advocacy" or "electioneering communications." That would be a dangerous route to censorship and governmental control over media. If BCRA was consistently enforced, the FEC would have to block MSNBC and Fox News from broadcasting news or commentary segments that favored or criticized a candidate by name within 30 days before a primary and 60 days before an election. This would effectively constitute a temporary news broadcast blackout in the run up to primaries and elections, except for public-owned media (PBS or NPR), newspapers and books, or the Internet. This idea may well be in the public's best interest and might improve the electoral process, but it hardly seems consistent with the First Amendment. A corporation would only need to purchase a newspaper or website and it could disseminate issue advocacy ads or electioneering communications in the guise of news and commentary, and there would be nothing the FEC could do about it.

Or,

(iii) The Fairness Doctrine needs to be respected by media corporations that take upon themselves the mantle of membership of "the press," and thereby warrant having special First Amendment protections not granted to other kinds of corporation. News corporations should limit their broadcasts during the run up to give statement of facts without commentary, respecting at least the appearance of impartiality when mentioning a candidate's name, unless that candidate is given a chance to exercise a right to reply. There is legal precedent for this, which Roberts et al. ignored.[27] Of course there will remain bias and "editorial discretion," but this would prevent the broadcast of attack ads during the run-up to primaries and elections, or at least would require media corporations to sell equal time to all the candidates and their advocates. This would be both measureable and verifiable, and would not favor the speech of any one party or individual over the others simply because they could pay for it.

Can we really consider speech to be free speech when someone is paid to say it? As well as failing to distinguish between free speech and paid-for speech—treating political speech (news and opinion) and political advertising (partisan attack ads and propaganda) as indistinguishable—Roberts *et al.* also seem to have ignored another important consequence of unlimited spending on electioneering communications and issue advocacy ads. Ad time is finite and there is an inflationary effect on the cost of producing and running such ads when increasing amounts of money are spent on them. This means that either more money is spent on political campaigns, and the more money it will cost to participate in the political process. Laws like BCRA effectively impose price controls. Without price controls, if the money supply increases then there is an inevitable inflationary vicious circle that with each reiteration further removes political speech from the reach of the majority of people, increases profits for media corporations, and intensifies the interdependency between politicians and money for election and re-election. The problem with SCOTUS's equation of speech with money is that it simply ignores the fact that the ability to spend more than others on commercially available media access prevents others from having equal access or any access at all. By rigging the system in favor of moneyed interests, this SCOTUS ruling has stifled the free speech of everyone else. It means that many categories of speakers will not be heard, just to protect only one category of speakers—purchasers of media access. Even if we put aside the concerns about propaganda and corruption, the majority decision to consider political speech in isolation has missed this crucial point. Allowing unlimited spending suppresses the right to free speech of people who cannot pay high prices for slots and segments on commercial media, and overwhelmingly favors the speech of those who can pay for it. This ruling dismisses out-of-hand the public interest in political equality, which is both vital to democracy and the legitimacy of the republican form of government, as a government that governs with the consent of the governed. The SCOTUS majority also ignored the fact that the airwaves are not private property, but owned by the public and licenses are issued to broadcasters by the FCC (as they have been since the 1934 Radio Act) on the condition they serve the public interest.[28] Laws that impose price controls on advertising slots during the run up to primaries and elections may well be a possible legislative solution to this problem, but, in my view, they would be more intrusive and draconian than BCRA's narrow restrictions, treating "the press" as a special category with rights and responsibilities, and respecting the fairness doctrine would be, and have less of a footing in the Constitution than Congress asserting its right to legislate campaign financing and the conduct of elections.

Of course, some people may argue that although propaganda and corruption are serious problems, abridging the right of corporations to pay for political speech is not the best way to deal with them. And I would agree with them. It should not matter where speech comes from and who pays for it. All forms of political censorship, no matter how well meaning, tend to end up justifying further censorship and media control. But in my view, we need more people enjoying the right to political speech, not fewer, and people do need to hear criticisms of politicians and policies no matter who pays for those criticisms to be made and aired. Media needs to be messy and biased. The real solutions comes from the people and the development of informed and critical thinking about how we interact with and learn from media, learning how to develop a critical relation with sources of information and how to analyze them; thereby fulfilling the people's role as an informed and enlightened electorate. The government does not facilitate democracy by telling the people what they can or cannot be told via broadcast media. But neither did the SCOTUS ruling. Rather than really representing a victory for every American who desires to participate in the political process, this ruling actually censors political speech by indirectly favoring only the representatives of corporate and moneyed interests.

Unlimited corporate spending on elections does limit and distort the First Amendment right of people to petition their government by making that right to do so conditional on paying enough money to get one's representative or senator elected or re-elected, and thereby making politicians beholden to their paymasters. Candidates from political parties, such as the Green Party, which does not accept money from corporate sponsors and opposes the corporate domination of America, will have their freedom of speech stifled even further as a result of this ruling; as will any third-party or independent candidates who also refuse money from corporate sponsors. Third Party candidates have an almost unsurmountable hurdle as it is against the established Democratic and Republican parties. With unlimited expenditures, a viable Third Party candidate has to match the spending of both of the established parties put together. Third Party candidates often struggle to get on the ballot and are rarely permitted by corporate media from having their voice broadcast or participating in televised debates. Ironically, BCRA may well have benefited incumbents, but the SCOTUS majority have entrenched the two-party system. Not only does the Citizens United ruling open the floodgates to corruption and cronyism, by allowing corporate money to saturate advertising during political campaigns, but corporate media can act as a powerful propaganda machine through the escalating costs of media access and propaganda campaigns by promoting only corporate interests, which manipulates the electorate by suppressing all dissenting views and by opposing candidates who oppose corporate interests (largely by shutting them out of media access), and slandering opposition without any right of reply. Issue advocacy ads selling the corporate agenda and discrediting opposition to that agenda are taking the place of anything resembling investigative journalism or a critical media watchdog. When mainstream news becomes indistinguishable from infomercials and political talking-points, it would be political suicide for politicians to oppose any laws corporate lobbyists wanted, let alone expose corruption and cronyism within the political system.[29] Far from aiding freedom of speech and the integrity of the political process, the SCOTUS majority have opened the door to a money-dominated system of revolving-door politics and aided the effectiveness of the propaganda machine to conceal itself behind the guise of free speech, while driving politics even deeper into corruption and cronyism.

This opens the door for the domination of election campaigns by highly sophisticated multi-platform, multi-media propaganda machines, comprised of seemingly independent but coordinated non-profits like Citizens United operating in concert with radio stations, newspapers, television channels, books, emails, magazines, social media and Internet sites. The SCOTUS majority should not have considered *Hillary: The Movie* in isolation. Citizens United Productions even boasts of this in its claim that it fulfils its mission by showing its movies and "targeted commercials" to a targeted audience, which is selected "based on the desired outcome, to maximize the impact of each dollar we spend."[30] Thus it largely appeals to an already partisan target audience, who pay to watch the CUP movies to further reinforce their worldview and confirm their suspicions, and to provide them with readymade "off the rack" refutations, boosting their immunity to alternative media and worldviews, especially those of the demonized opposition: the Democratic Party and "the Left."[31] Elsewhere, I have termed this kind of audience as being *narrowcasted*: suspicious of any source of media that contradicts or challenges their prejudices or worldview, and only willing to accept opinions that reinforce and confirm their prejudices and worldview from a narrowly selected and coordinated sources.[32] Obviously these movies appeal to the party faithful and they contribute to maintaining support for the party, and there is nothing wrong with that, but by being so narrowcasted and partisan they also allow double-standards to be practiced without scrutiny or criticism. Hence, despite celebrating the SCOTUS ruling as upholding free speech and portraying it as a David v Goliath struggle,[33] Citizens United's director David Bossie could shamelessly criticize Barack Obama during the 2012 presidential campaign for embracing Super PACs.[34] Apparently, only Republicans should do that.

Rather than helping voters make informed choices and giving all candidates access to media and the political process, the SCOTUS ruling has marginalized and silenced candidates that do not represent corporate interests and do not have corporate financial backing. This state of affairs makes Third Party and independent candidates appear as "a wasted vote," if they appear on the ballot at all, and allows corporate media to act as gate-keepers and exclude candidates from participating in debates and being heard by the electorate, as well as narrowing the range of issues and concerns raised during election campaigns to those that suit corporate interests, especially when Third Party and independent candidates are more often than not shut out of the debates. The SCOTUS majority have made any obstacle to the domination of corporate money to be unconstitutional and illegal by definition. Henceforth, political candidates will either have vast sums of independent wealth or they will be beholden to corporate sponsors. This not only further entrenches the two-party system, but brings the parties together to only represent a narrow range of corporate interests. If the candidates from both the Democratic Party and the Republican Party represent only corporate interests, America becomes a one-party state with two wings: the Corporate America Party.[35] The differences between the Democratic and Republican wings of CAP, say on same-sex marriage, abortion, or gun control, become distractions and wedge issues to present the illusion of substantive differences, and conceal from the electorate the extent that the candidates otherwise share the same plutocratic agenda and serve the same moneyed interests. At best, elections become a struggle between competing cartels of corporations, struggling for differences in the regulatory environment that favor them rather than their competitors, so some industries tend to favor the Democrats (pharmaceuticals and telecoms, for example) and others tend to favor the Republicans (big oil, coal and gas), but often both candidates will receive money from many the same corporations (Wall Street, private prisons, and the arms manufacturers), and use wedge issues to raise donations from special interest groups and individuals. Voting (assuming that the votes are even counted) becomes a ritualistic process of mass media deception and public manipulation to present the illusion of democratic participation and the legitimation of the outcomes of the political process, while the outcome of "the election" would be effectively decided by media corporations on behalf of a parent or holding corporation. The "winner" will be the highest bidder.

Another problem ignored by the SCOTUS majority ruling is the problem of media consolidation. Since the 1996 Telecoms Act, which deregulated much of the telecommunications industry and lifted restrictions on cross-media ownership and media consolidation, mass media has become owned by fewer and fewer people.[36] Today, 90% of all U.S. television and radio stations are owned by six corporations: Comcast (which owns NBC Universal, Weather Channel, etc.), Walt Disney (ABC, Buena Vista, A&E, etc.) News Corporation (Fox News, DirecTV, Harper Collins, etc.), Time Warner (which owns CNN etc.), and National Amusements (which owns Viacom and CBS, which owns Simon & Schuster, etc.). They do have some competition. Bertelsmann (a foreign investment group which owns Random House, Penguin, etc.) and the Hearst Corporation, along with News Corporation (Harper Collins) own the majority of American newspapers, magazines, and publishing houses, and Bain Capital's Clear Channel Communications owns a growing majority of radio stations in America (including the Premiere Radio Network). Through acquisitions and mergers, media holdings have become the property of increasingly larger conglomerates until they became the giants of today. After General Electric sold Comcast its stock in NBC Universal, Comcast became a massive telecoms and media conglomerate, owning both media content and its infrastructure for transmission and reception. Since 2014, Comcast has sought to acquire Time Warner, which would make it the majority owner of telecommunications, wireless, and broadband in America, effectively giving it control over Internet access, as well as news, information, and entertainment media for over 60% of the American population. The remaining share of telecoms, wireless, and broadband are divided between AT&T, Cablevision, CenturyLink, Charter, Sprint Nextel, T-Mobile (a subsidiary of the German company Deutsche Telekom), and Verizon.

How can we expect politicians and their appointees to stand by and enforce antitrust legislation when their election and re-election depends on the owners of the very same conglomerate that seeks the repeal of that legislation and further deregulation of its industry? Comcast lobbyists and Super PACs have been working hard on trying to overcome the pesky hurdles of anti-trust legislation and the restrictions as enforced by the Federal Communications Commission (FCC), staffed by former executives and board members of the very industry they are supposed to regulate. By the time you are reading these words, "the Big Six" are likely to be "the Big Five." It is only a matter of time before these too merge into one or are bought up or squeezed out by Comcast. Or maybe Comcast, or any or all of the others, will be bought out by some larger investment group. Increasingly, corporations like Comcast are becoming the gate-keepers of communications, information, and the electoral process. This gives them enormous power and this power is exercised for the benefit of shareholders rather than the good of the general public, especially when it comes to deciding on prices, upgrading infrastructure, and controlling the rate of data transmission.

How can this situation of increased media consolidation help increase diversity of media ownership and control, and facilitate a culture of truly independent expenditures and a genuinely free press? It does not seem likely. The SCOTUS majority ruling has effectively made the media beholden to corporate interests, and thereby handed over the task of safeguarding the integrity of the free press and electoral process to those corporate interests. SCOTUS has placed the onus on Congress to regulate use existing antitrust legislation or write new legislation to break up media conglomerates into smaller companies, prevent cross-media ownership, or at least prevent the simultaneous ownership of communications infrastructure and content. This seems a labor of Sisyphus in comparison to the much more modest one in comparison with legislating campaign expenditure limits and broadcast restrictions in the run-up to primaries and elections.

Congress does have a number of options.

(1) Congress can use its constitutional power as given in Article I, Section 4 and Article III, section 2, without requiring any amendment to the Constitution, to either overrule SCOTUS, or to censure and threaten to impeach the SCOTUS majority for judicial activism and their jurisdiction in breach of their oath of office. Congress could assert its constitutional authority to legislate elections and force SCOUTUS to remain within its jurisdiction as defined by Article III of the Constitution. There is no constitutional mechanism by which SCOTUS could prevent the impeachment and replacement of SCOTUS justices if Congress deems that the court has breached the separation of powers and exceeded its jurisdiction by interfering with election law and preventing Congress from protecting the integrity of the political process. Of course, this is unlikely to happen. This remedy is likely to fall afoul of the extent to which Congress is already beholden to corporations, and, in the unlikely event it happened at all, under the pressure of lobbyists, the complexity of the legislative process would be used either to stall the legislative process or create enough loopholes such that it would not serve as much of a remedy at all.

(2) Congress could do what it has done for the last 150 years and write new legislation in response to SCOTUS that can make another attempt at getting comprehensive campaign financing reform right and respecting the First Amendment. First Amendment violations can be avoided if restrictions are narrowly tailored *to the medium and timeframe of broadcast of political speech, rather than its content or the identity of the speaker*. However, again we see how beholden Congress is to corporate money. We can see how this problem reared its head after, in response to the Citizens United ruling, Senator Charles E. Schumer (D—NY) and Representative Chris Van Hollen (D—MD) introduced

the DISCLOSE Act in the Senate and House in April, 2010 to overturn the SCOTUS decision. This law would have required additional disclosure of corporate expenditures and prevented government contractors and companies with 20% or more foreign ownership from political spending. On June 24, HR 5175 passed the House (after amendments and exemptions had been written into the DISCLOSE Act) but it twice failed to avoid the threat of filibuster the Senate, even after a much weakened version had been passed in the House.

(3) Congress could tighten the regulations and broaden the enforcement powers of the FCC and FEC in order to give them real teeth and better protect the public interest. The President could nominate and Congress approve commissioners that opposed media consolidation and deregulation, and ensure that broadcast license holders act in the public interest. In fact the reverse has happened, and chairmen to the FCC, such as Thomas Wheeler and his predecessor Julius Genachowski, have been telecom industry insiders who favor deregulation.

(4) Congress could avoid a constitutional crisis or conflict with the Supreme Court by amending the Revenue Act and rewrite the tax code. Congress can set strict limits to the tax deduction of donations, and lobbying and campaign expenditures. Corporations could spend however much they wanted on issue advocacy ads and electioneering communications, and lobbying, but could not deduct these as expenses from the tax bill. This would place something of a break on campaign spending in general. Congress could also pass a law requiring shareholder consent before corporate funds are spent on political speech or campaign contributions. SCOTUS could not rule either as a violation of the First Amendment.

(5) Congress and the Executive could create a constitutional crisis in a rather interesting manner. The Constitution does not specify how many judges sit on the Supreme Court. Nine has been established by convention and tradition, but not by the Constitution. It is possible for the President to nominate and for Congress to approve the number of judges (as President Franklin Delano Roosevelt threatened to do, as a result of the SCOTUS of his time practically striking down every piece of legislation pertaining to labor and the regulation of commerce). Perhaps it is time to raise the question of whether more justices need to sit on the bench of SCOTUS. But given the difficulty in even getting Congress to approve nominations for long-standing vacancies for federal judges, this seems an unlikely path for Congress to take. Maybe it is time to consider whether SCOTUS justices should be elected. Perhaps Congress should even declare by law that every citizen over 65 years of age is a Justice of the Supreme Court of the United States of America, with the sole requirement that they can demonstrate that they have read the Constitution, and draw nine at random from this pool to preside over any particular case.

(6) Amend the Constitution to clarify that the enumerated rights belong to natural persons, not corporations, and follow that up with new campaign finance reform to remove the dominance of corporate money in political campaigns.[37] Some members of Congress have taken notice. Donna Edwards, Leonard Boswell, John Kerry, and Bernie Sanders, for example, have all called for constitutional

amendments to abolish corporate personhood and overturn this ruling. There are also other reasons why a constitutional amendment to abolish corporate personhood would benefit the General Welfare of the people, but, in the context of Citizens United it affords a clear and meaningful campaign through which the people of different political persuasions can become involved in the political process, which is itself a requirement for a healthy democracy, to pressure Congress and the States to convene a national conventions to write, pass, and ratify this amendment, and, by doing so, assert the sovereignty of the people. This affords the people an opportunity to affirm and continue the American Revolution and the experiment in self-governance. It is an opportunity for transparency, accountability, and legitimacy of government to be seen to be achieved of the people, for the people, and by the people—government by the consent of the governed—as part of the ongoing fulfillment of the promise of the *Declaration of Independence* and the American Revolution. The renewal of the public faith in the political process can be achieved if the people stand up together as "we the people" and demand that the government represents them and protects their constitutional rights. And, of course, once it is made clear to SCOTUS that the enumerated rights belong to natural persons, not corporations, it will be possible for Congress to reestablish its own constitutional authority over elections and to limit the jurisdiction of SCOTUS accordingly, and, thereby, pass and enforce effective campaign financing reform legislation to get money out of politics and prevent the corruption of elections and the political process.

(7) States can amend their constitutions and call on Congress to convene a National Convention. A number of States, including California, Hawaii, Vermont, Rhode Island, Maryland, New Mexico, New York, Washington, and Massachusetts have all passed resolutions calling for the Citizens United decision to be overturned. This seems the most likely path. Once three-quarters of States agree on calling a National Convention, Congress will be compelled by Article V of the Constitution to do it.

(8) Congress could fund the further develop the online presence of national public media, making PBS and NPR streaming and downloads available via a public ISP that can offset the cost of political campaigning for candidates and allow greater access for third party and independent candidates. The U.S. Postal Service could run this public ISP, updating Congress's Article I duty "to establish the Post Office and Post roads" in the context of the Internet, which was invented by AARPA from funds granted by Congress, and could offer low price Internet access to the public, schools and public libraries, public wireless, protect net neutrality, and also raise revenues for the Postal Service by users of the service.[38] The FCC should continue to classify the Internet as a utility and recognize its importance for communications and elections. The Internet should be used as the means through which people can create their own free press, as a democratic media, and organize grassroots campaign to run for public office. People need to actively seek out independent sources of information, check the facts for themselves, and have a broader framework of debate available to them.

None of these measures would oppress anyone's free speech. Non-profit corporations and advocacy groups—however funded—would be able to air their electioneering communications and advocacy ads on private and public media. By restricting the flow of money into politics and media, more people will gain access to media, especially non-moneyed interests. If a condition of gaining the status and constitutional protection of "the press," media corporations should not be beholden to parent or holding corporations. Restrictions on cross-owning media, says television stations and newspapers, also should be tightened and enforced. This limitation is not be a limitation of speech, but a limit on the ownership of the means for one's speech to be heard. This limitation is justified not only if we recognize of the validity of the claim that broadcast media is more amenable to disseminating propaganda, but also in the democratic need for media to represent a wide spectrum of interests and biases. It is therefore in the public interest to (a) place limits on how that medium can be used when the public interest is at stake; (b) pressure the government to break up media conglomerates through antitrust legislation; (c) have a good coverage of and access to the political process via public media; (d) have reliable and affordable access to the Internet; and (e) have access to diverse and independent media sources. Rather than stifling debate, this would increase public participation through public television and radio, and Internet-based media, and actually improve the quality of public debate and democracy.

The public does not need to be shielded from the onslaught of broadcast propaganda for or against candidates during elections and primaries, providing that the public has access to and control over diverse and independent media. The electorate needs to be afforded the opportunity to seek out information about candidates and commentary from diverse and independent sources, and produce their own free press, using the Internet and public media, as well as being able to watch news on corporate TV and radio channels, and buying and reading their choice of newspaper. This involves more media—greater media diversity—as well as good public education in critical thinking and research skills. The public needs to learn the recognize propaganda, and use the Internet and learn how to be the free press of the people, from the people, and for the people.[39]

Media corporations and their parent corporations have benefited most from the SCOTUS majority ruling, largely at the expense of the public faith in the integrity of the electoral process. With the creation of Super PACs, the bidding for ad time reached record highs during the 2012 election campaign, and these records will almost certainly be eclipsed by the 2016 election campaign. Soon only those wealthy citizens who can outbid multinational corporations out of their own pockets will be able to participate in electioneering communications on corporate owned TV and radio, and the Internet. The SCOTUS majority have transformed the nature of the political process into one of a perpetual lobbying machine and revolving door that corrupts government and remove all legislative obstacles to the maximization of corporate profits for shareholders. The SCOTUS ruling has taken America one step closer to becoming a corporate state by creating the political superstructure of a corporate state. Corporations will necessarily lobby for a favorable regulatory environment, the lowest labor costs, and access to cheap natural resources, regardless of the social and environmental consequences. Given that it is a matter of law that corporations pursue profits for shareholders, rather than the interests of the citizenry, once national and corporate interests are one and the same thing, America will become a full-fledged corporate state with access to the largest military force in the world. Corporations can also use private armed forces to further corporate interests, without any governmental oversight or legal consequences. Increasingly the government is dependent on corporations to provide services and conduct the operations of government. Now that SCOTUS has turned the political process into an instrument of corporate dominance over society, corporations can also use the police as a paramilitary force to suppress dissent and opposition among the citizenry, and increasingly the law will place corporate interests over the interests of the people. Without politicians acting on behalf of the people to restore the balance between government and corporate power, there is nothing to stop the inevitable political disenfranchisement of the people and the rise of the corporate state.

It is for this reason that the majority ruling in Citizens United v FEC, 2010, was catastrophic for democracy in America. It remains to be seen whether Congress is too beholden to corporations to be pressured by the people to do something to reverse this, or whether "we, the people" are up the proverbial creek without a paddle. Will Congress put the democratic interests of the people before the interests of corporations? Will the people put their own democratic interests over and above the promise of jobs and cheap consumer goods? Will the electorate stand up and pressure Congress to act in the interests of all the people and not just those people associated in corporate form? If the people do not compel their representatives to represent them, and participate in the political process, only the people who are funding the election and reelection of politicians will be the people who have any say whatsoever on who is elected and what they do once they are. Ultimately, this comes down to the question of who are the electorate in America… corporations or all the people? Who does America belong to?

---

[1] Reproduced in Karl Rogers, *Propaganda and the Free Press* (Los Angeles, CA: Trébol Press, 2016)

[2] Citizens United v. Federal Election Commission, 558 U.S. 08-205 (2010).

[3] See the official homepage of *Hillary: The Movie* http://www.hillarythemovie.com/ .

[4] Congressional Quarterly Weekly Report, Vol. xxvii, No. 49, December 5, 1969, p. 2435; Clerk of the House, "The Annual Statistical Report of Contributions and Expenditures Made During the 1972 Election Campaigns for the U.S. House of Representatives" (1974), p. 161; Secretary of the Senate, "The Annual Statistical Report of Receipts and Expenditures Made in connection with Elections for the U.S. Senate in 1972" [undated], p. 33.

[5] FEC data http://www.fec.gov/disclosure.shtml http://www.fec.gov/pdf/ar80.pdf
Campaign Finance Institute http://www.cfinst.org/data/historicalstats.aspx#President

[6] http://www.cfinst.org/pdf/vital/VitalStats_t2.pdf

[7] http://www.cfinst.org/pdf/vital/VitalStats_t5.pdf

[8] http://www.cfinst.org/pdf/vital/VitalStats_t9.pdf

[9] The text of the majority opinion in this case can be found at the Supreme Court website: http://www.supremecourt.gov/opinions/09pdf/08-205.pdf. Transcripts for this case can also be found at

Oyez (a Chicago-Kent multimedia archive of Supreme Court rulings) http://www.oyez.org/cases/2000-2009/2008/2008_08_205#opinion.

[10] Stare decisis is the legal principle by which judges are obliged to respect the precedents established by prior decisions. The words originate from the phrasing of the principle in the Latin maxim Stare decisis et non quieta movere: "to stand by decisions and not disturb the rested." In a legal context, this is understood to mean that courts should generally abide by precedents and not disturb settled matters.

[11] See CU website: http://citizensunited.org/

[12] Center for Responsive Politics
 http://www.opensecrets.org/pacs/lookup2.php?strID=C00295527&cycle=2004
and Follow The Money
http://www.followthemoney.org/press/ReportView.phtml?r=414&gclid=CLeQpeT-va4CFQKEhwodrSbJSQ

[13] http://citizensunited.org/what-we-do.aspx

[14] In Regan v Taxation With Representation, 1983, the Supreme Court ruled that the IRS prohibition of 501(c)(3) non-profit organizations from supporting political campaigns was not in violation of the First Amendment.

[15] ABC showed the miniseries *Path to 9/11*—a dramatization in two parts—on September 10th and 11th 2006. About 25 million people watched it. To be fair, the plot of the second part also implicates the Bush Administration for being woefully ill prepared and caught napping.

[16] Steve Chapman, "Free speech, even for corporations." *Chicago Tribune Opinion*, Jan, 24, 2010

[17] Ironically, the ACLU is the subject of a Citizens United movie *ACLU: At War With America* that portrays the ACLU as a threat to America and its most basic values.

[18] Ford v Dodge Motor Company, 1919. The Michigan Supreme Court held that Henry Ford had a legal obligation to maximize profits for shareholders, over any other consideration, such as the community or the workers. (And, over and above the environment and the integrity of the political process too).

[19] John Coates, *Corporate Governance and Corporate Political Activity: What Effect Will Citizens United Have on Shareholder Wealth?* (Harvard Law and Economics Discussion Paper No. 684, 2010)

[20] Schenck v United States, 1919; Abrams v United States, 1919; Dennis v United States, 1951; Miller v California, 1973; Osborne v Ohio, 1990; Barnes v Glen Theater, 1991

[21] Rob Hager and James Marc Leas, "The Problem With Citizens United Is Not Corporate Personhood" *Truthout*, Jan, 17, 2012; James Marc Leas, "Constitutional Amendment Not Needed: Congress Already Has a Remedy", *Truthout*, Jan, 17, 2012; Kent Greenfield "Why Progressives Should Oppose A Constitutional Amendment to End Corporate Personhood" *Huffington Post*, Jan, 26, 2012 http://www.huffingtonpost.com/kent-greenfield/why-progressives-should-o_b_1231884.html
For an interesting discussion of these articles see Victor Tiffany, "Taking on amendment critics," parts I and II, *Abolish Corporate Personhood Now*, Feb, 29, 2012
 http://abolishcorporatepersonhoodnow.org/2012/02/29/taking-on-amendment-critics-part-i-james-marc-leas-and-rob-hagar/

[22] For more details and further discussion see Karl Rogers, Propaganda and the Free Press (Los Angeles, CA: Trébol Press, 2016), chapter 3.

[23] Since Beauharnais v. Illinois, 1952, the Supreme Court has upheld that racial slurs count as group slander when published. Milkovich v Lorain Journal Co, 1990, the Supreme Court ruled that slander was not protected under the First Amendment because statements of objective fact can be checked and are not opinions. Yet, since Philadelphia Newspapers v Hepps,, 1986, the onus is on the plaintiff to prove falsity and libel. And, in McDonald v Smith, 1985, the Supreme Court ruled that the First Amendment right to petition does not provide protection of libelous statements, but, in Bose v Consumers Union, 1984, and New York Times v Sullivan, 1964, the plaintiff has to show "intended malice", or at least "neglect", as in Gertz v Welch, 1974. Although, in Hustler Magazine v Falwell, 1988, the Supreme Court ruled that public figures could not claim emotional distress when any reasonable person could tell the difference between parody and statements of fact.

[24] Some organizations, such as Common Cause, have questioned the impartiality of Scalia and Thomas and have pointed out conflicts of interest. http://www.commoncause.org/

[25] See Chapter 4 of my *Propaganda and the Free Press* for further details and discussion.

[26] Grosjean v American Press, 1936; Burstyn v Wilson, 1952; Freedman v Maryland, 1965; New York Times v United States, 1971; Kois v Wisconsin, 1972; Branzburg v Hayes, 1972; Miami Herald Publishing Co. v Tornillo, 1976; Gertz v Welch, 1976; Zurcher v. Stanford Daily, 1978 (leading to Congress passing the 1980 Privacy Protection Act, further protecting press freedom); Minneapolis Star Tribune Company v Commissioner, 1983; Bose v Consumers Union, 1984; Philadelphia Newspapers v Hepps, 1986; Press-Enterprise v Superior Court, 1986; Hazelwood v Kuhlmeier, 1988; Hustler Magazine v Falwell, 1988; Milkovich v Lorain, 1990; Simon & Schuster v Crime Victims Board, 1991; Cincinnati v Discovery Network, 1993

[27] Red Lion Broadcasting v FCC, 1969

[28] See Turner Broadcasting v FCC, 1994 for the extension of this to cable TV.

[29] David Kirkpatrick, "Lobbyists Get Potent Weapon in Campaign Financing." *The New York Times*, Jan, 22, 2010

[30] http://citizensunited.org/fulfilling-our-mission.aspx

[31] Citizens United's movie *Occupy Unmasked*—released in 2012 and posthumously featuring the late Andrew Breibart's exposé of "the true story about the radicals behind the Occupy movement" as a sinister movement of anarchists and communists rather than American citizens seeking to petition their government, as is their First Amendment constitutional right.

[32] Karl Rogers, *Debunking Glenn Beck: How to Save America from Media Pundits and Propagandists* (Santa Barbara, CA: Praeger, 2011)

[33] http://cuvfec.com/

[34] http://www.citizensunited.org/latest-updates.aspx?article=4930

[35] See David Samuels, *False Choice: The Bipartisan Attack on the Working Class, the Poor, and Communities of Color* (Los Angeles, CA: Trébol Press)

[36] See Chapter 2.

[37] I have discussed this route in detail elsewhere. See *Debunking Glenn Beck*, chapter 12, and *Occupy Media!* (2012)

[38] See Chapter 2 of my *Propaganda and the Free Press* for further details and discussions.

[39] See Chapter 3 and 4 of my *Propaganda and the Free Press* for further details and discussion.

www.ingramcontent.com/pod-product-compliance
Lightning Source LLC
Chambersburg PA
CBHW080644190526
45169CB00009B/3490